• • •

The Fatherhood Crisis

The Fatherhood Crisis

The Effects on Children Who Do Not Have A Positive Father-Child Attachment

Dr. Noel Casiano

ISBN-13: 9781548160951
ISBN-10: 1548160954

In loving memory of my grandfather (Abuelo):
Don Pablo Torres
Although not perfect, you were the first male
role model in my life.

Table of Content

Acknowledgments

My love and appreciation goes out to my wife, Yecenia, and awesome son, Nick. They have given me the support and inspiration to achieve the publication of this book. They are ultimately the main reason I get up every morning and try to make a small difference in this world—so that they also can enjoy a lifetime of love and support. I learned a long time ago how important family is, but your relationship has only affirmed how much you both mean to me. From the bottom of my heart, I love you both and thank you for your unconditional love.

To my mom, who raised me and my sister as a single mother: Know that you did your best under the many difficult circumstances without my father.

I am eternally grateful, Mom, for your sacrifices that you endured willingly for our family.

To my siblings, Beatrice, Bobby, Ariel, and Amarilis: We had our own experiences with Dad, and we are who we are today due to our own resilience and hard work. Continue to strive to be who you are, because God has blessed us with one another.

Also, to my faith family at House of Restoration Church: Thank you for your support and unconditional love while entrusting me in the leadership of your Pastoral Counseling Center. Thank you, Bishop Jeremiah Torres and Senior Pastor Miriam Torres, for your kind words of encouragement, trust, and guidance. My church family inspires me to continue this important work and research.

Dedication

This book is dedicated to those children who did not have the opportunity to have a positive relationship with their father. May you find the inner healing that you so dearly deserve and ultimately, if possible, establish a paternal relationship. Also, may those fathers who desire to have a relationship with their children please find the strength and resources to reestablish a father-child relationship as soon as possible. Your children desperately need it.

Chapter 1

●　●　●

The Fatherhood Crisis

*"I cannot think of any need in
childhood as strong as the need
for a father's protection"*

- SIGMUND FREUD

The purpose of this book is to review past and current literature on secure attachment, specifically the attachment between a father and his child. In the past years, the importance of father-child attachment, father involvement, and child-development concerns have been one area of interest within the field of psychology and child development. Paternal engagement has received increased attention in recent years because of its impact on positive development outcomes for children. There has been noted impact of father-child secure attachment on healthy child development, academic achievement, emotional and psychological functioning in children, and legal and delinquency issues among children who do not have a secure father-child attachment or father involvement.

In regard to recent research findings in neuroscience, it is important to note the relational impacts on children's well-being as well. Neuroscience findings point to the need for healthy relational bonding between children and their parents. When fathers are not present or available to meet the relational needs of their children, the brain stem, midbrain, limbic brain, and prefrontal cortex are all negatively affected in many different ways. Therefore, this book will review past research along with current studies to understand the impact of secure and insecure father-child attachment and the impact of father involvement or lack of involvement on children.

• • •

Background of the Problem

Researchers have found implications for children who do not have good or secure attachment bonds with their biological father. Bowlby's attachment theory (Bowlby 1982) suggests that adaptive patterns of parent-child interaction in the early years promote the development of secure relationships between children and their caregivers. As such, this early relationship can serve as a source of emotional security that promotes healthy functioning across many domains of development.

For example, in looking at emotional factors of secure father-child attachment, it has been found that securely attached children show fewer behavioral problems, greater sociability, and more reciprocated friendships than those in insecure relationships. Indeed, father-child attachment security appears to be important for children's nonclinical outcomes and may lower their risks for internalizing and externalizing forms of psychopathology (Brown, Mangelsdorf, and Neff 2012).

In assessing psychological impacts on male children who had no secure father-child attachment, parental bonding styles of the father were significantly more causative of suicide ideation in contrast to males who had optimal bonding with their fathers. Also, perceived parental bonding style was found to be significantly related to several indicators of distress among incarcerated adolescents. For both males and females, hopelessness was found to be significantly associated with a bonding style with the opposite-sex parent (McGarvey et al. 1999).

Children possessing father hunger may encounter low self-esteem, fear of abandonment, exaggerated feelings of loneliness, and shame. They also may experience counter dependence, problems managing emotions or anger, need for control, and problems involving trust. Also, these children are more likely to be diagnosed with substance abuse, depression, schizophrenia, and eating disorders (Perrin et al. 2009).

When looking at educational impacts on children without secure attachments with their father, it has been found that in middle childhood, father involvement was positively associated with greater academic achievement and enjoyment of school (Garfield and Isacco 2012). It was also found that the father's availability and involvement were associated with cognitive gains and academic success in school-aged children, including higher grades and achievement in math and reading (Howard et al. 2006). Also, a higher level of paternal involvement in their children's schools was associated with better grades, fewer suspensions, and lower dropout rates than were lower levels of involvement (Kelly and Lamb 2003).

Children with no father involvement or no secure father-child attachment will struggle with issues of poverty. This is because these children grow up primarily in a single-parent, single-income home (Geary 2000). High levels of paternal investment, such as income and playtime, are typically correlated with better child outcomes—for example, improved social and academic skills and higher socioeconomic status in adulthood (Geary 2000). Children living in a one-parent household will not be able to benefit from two income sources for the family.

When looking at biological and sexual development, it has been noted that father absence has unique effects on female sexual outcomes but not on male sexual outcomes (James et al. 2012). For girls only, father absence directly and uniquely predicts earlier timing of sexual debut and greater sexual risk taking. It also has a significant indirect effect on earlier pubertal maturation through quality of family relationships and has a significant indirect effect on increased sexual risk taking through earlier sexual debut. In addition, in both girls and boys, father absence has a significant indirect effect on earlier sexual debut through lower quality of family relationships (James et al. 2012). Also, risk factors such as high family conflict, abuse, parental psychopathology, and divorce can serve to establish enduring dysregulations in the child's psychological stress response, promoting pathophysiology in the brain and body and contributing to hypertension, heart disease, infectious disease, and other illnesses (Fabricius and Luecken 2007).

Lastly, father absence or insecure father-child attachment was found to be associated with negative child outcomes, including increased risk for deviant behavior and delinquency. In a study of children ages five to eighteen, father involvement decreased behavioral problems and positively contributed to social competence (Garfield and Isacco 2012).

• • •

Statement of the Problem

I will examine the role and importance of secure father-child attachment bonds. If children have a secure father-child attachment bond, they will be able to enjoy a healthy relationship with their father. If a secure father-child bond is not achieved, then the children will be exposed to many negative factors that will impact their developmental process, educational and academic achievement, emotional and psychological health, and tendency toward substance abuse. Furthermore, they will be at risk with regard to illegal activity and delinquency issues. I will look at father-child attachment bonds in both single-parent and two-parent homes.

• • •

Purpose

The purpose of this book is to investigate the impact on children who do not have a secure father-child attachment. According to Bowlby's attachment theory (1982), if a child does not have a secure father-child attachment or relationship with his or her father, the child will struggle with many negative clinical implications. The focus of this project will primarily be on the father-child attachment and the effects of not having a secure father-child attachment on children. These results and clinical research findings will be discussed in order to provide information that can be used in assessing and treating children, adolescents, and adults who have experienced insecure father-child attachment.

• • •

Theoretical Framework

This book will discuss John Bowlby's attachment theory in order to create a foundation of the importance of a healthy parent-child and father-child attachment. Through the collective work of John Bowlby and Mary Ainsworth, attachment theory emerged in the 1960s as a novel perspective on early personality formation. Drawing upon a rich mixture of ideas from evolution and systems theories, ethology, and cognitive science, Bowlby became an advocate. He proposed that attachment, or the human propensity to seek proximity to caregivers during moments of discomfort or threat, functioned as an independent, innate, and enduring motivational system. It was designed by natural selection to serve the survival needs of the young and thus to advance their ultimate reproductive success (Mattanah, Lopez, and Govern 2011).

When infants experience their primary caregivers as consistently warm, accessible, and responsive to their bids for care and support, a secure attachment bond is presumed to form, enabling the parent-child relationship to serve as a safe haven when the child experiences threats or frustrations that activate the attachment system. Distress is alleviated, and the system returns to a quiescent state.

On the other hand, if caregivers are experienced as inconsistently responsive to or consistently rejecting of the infant's natural proximity-seeking needs, an insecure parent-child attachment bond will likely form (Mattanah, Lopez, and Govern 2011).

• • •

Questions to Be Explored

The questions that I will explore are as follows: How does a lack of father-child attachment affect child development? How does a lack of father-child attachment affect a child's academic achievement? How does a lack of father-child attachment affect emotional and psychological functioning? Lastly, how does a lack of father-child attachment become a risk factor for legal or delinquency issues?

• • •

Importance of Fatherhood

Mental health practitioners and providers have contact with many children and adults who have psychological, emotional, educational, and legal issues. This book will serve as another resource to understand the impact of how fatherlessness and insecure

father-child attachment affect the overall functioning of these children and adults. Another purpose
of this book is to find answers by reviewing clinical
implications and recommendations that were made
in various studies. This information will assist mental health professionals in the assessment and understanding of children and adults who struggle with
insecure father-child attachment. This book will
include clinical recommendations and discuss limi-
tations for individuals who struggle with insecure
father-child attachment. Also, it will highlight how
this insecure father-child attachment has affected
their individual and family lives.

I will examine past and current journal and
research articles that address issues on how insecure
father-child and parent-child attachment affects the
domains of child development, academic achievement, emotional and psychological functioning, and
legal and delinquency issues. Many research studies have been conducted since the introduction of
Bowlby's attachment theory, which will help in
understanding the impact of insecure father-child
attachment.

My hope is that by reviewing what has been
found in past research studies, we can compare and
contrast the different clinical and social impacts on

father-child attachment. Individuals who will benefit from these results and findings are children and adults who have experienced insecure father-child attachment, mental health providers, and mental health researchers.

Bowlby's attachment theory's primary focus was on mother-child attachment. Therefore, many of the studies conducted refer to mother-child attachment issues and concerns. I will review and share various findings that focus on father-child attachment in order to provide data for the research questions that are being addressed throughout this study. Father-child attachment provides a set of clinically significant implications that are different from mother-child attachment. Therefore, this study will separate mother-child attachment from father-child attachment and provide a research base to address and highlight the implications of father-child attachment and father involvement.

● ● ●

Chapter 2

● ● ●

Implications of Father-Child Attachment

"The quality of a father can be seen in the goals, dreams and aspirations he sets not only for himself, but for his family."

—REED MARKHAM

This book will look at the implications for children who do not have a secure father-child attachment. Research has revealed that when children do not have a secure father-child attachment, negative implications can be seen in the areas of attachment, child development, academic achievement, emotional and psychological functioning, and risk of legal and delinquency involvement. Many of the attachment studies that have been conducted focused primarily on mother-child attachment bonds. Also, father involvement, defined as what and how much a father does for the child, has been the central area of study in fathering research for the past thirty years (Garfield and Isacco 2012). I will use Bowlby's attachment theory as the basis for all analysis.

Attachment theory, developed by Bowlby, highlights the influence of early, close relationships between infant and caregiver. Secure infant-caregiver attachment relationships provide good foundations for children's later socioemotional development, including greater social competence, greater conscience development, and fewer internalizing and externalizing problems. The positive associations between secure attachment and later functioning highlight the need to understand the origins of attachment relationships. According to Bowlby, the quality of early care that infants receive has important implications for the development of attachment security. Although it has been well documented that infants form attachment relationships with fathers as well as with mothers, most of the past research examining the antecedents of infant-parent attachment relationships has focused on infant-mother dyads. The role of fathers as attachment figures, however, should not be underestimated, as recent research has found that father involvement is associated with a range of favorable child outcomes (Wong et al. 2009).

The father's quality of involvement has important implications for infant-father attachment. It was found that fathers who reported greater engagement in child caretaking tasks also described their infants as more secure. Also, it was found that fathers' observed positive interactions with infants were associated with greater infant-father attachment security in the Strange Situation.

Psychologist Mary Ainsworth devised the Strange Situation procedure to test the quality of an infant's attachment to his mother. To test a child's "attachment style," researchers put the child and her mother (because these studies almost always focus on the mother) alone in an experimental room.

The room has toys or other interesting things in it, and the mother lets the child explore the room on her own. After the child has had time to explore, a stranger enters the room and talks with the mother. Then the stranger shifts attention to the child. As the stranger approaches the child, the mother sneaks away. After several minutes, the mother returns. She comforts her child and then leaves again. The stranger leaves as well. A few minutes later, the stranger returns and interacts with the child. Finally, the mother returns and greets her child.

• • •

Attachment styles in children
Securely attached children

The securely attached child explores the room freely when Mom is present. The child may be distressed when his or her mother leaves, and he or she explores less when she is absent, but the child is once again happy when she returns. If the child cries, the child approaches his or her mother and holds her tightly. The child is comforted by being held, and, once comforted, the child is soon ready to resume his or her independent exploration of the world. This child's mother is responsive to her child's needs. As a result, the child knows that he or she can depend on her when the child is under stress (Ainsworth et al. 1978).

• • •

Avoidant-insecure children

The avoidant-insecure child doesn't explore much, and the child doesn't show much emotion when the mother leaves. The child shows no preference for his or her mother over a complete stranger. And, when the mother returns, the child tends to avoid or ignore her (Ainsworth et al. 1978).

• • •

Resistant-insecure children

Like the avoidant child, the resistant-insecure child doesn't explore much on their own. Unlike the avoidant child, the resistant child is wary of strangers and is very distressed when their mother leaves. When the mother returns, the resistant child is ambivalent. Although the child wants to reestablish close proximity to their mother, this child is also resentful—even angry—at their mother for leaving them in the first place. As a result, the resistant child may reject her mother's advances (Ainsworth et al. 1978).

• • •

Disorganized-insecure children

The disorganized child may exhibit a mix of avoidant and resistant behaviors. But the main theme is one of confusion and anxiety. Disorganized-insecure children are at risk for a variety of behavioral and developmental problems. This is because of their lack of positive attachment and relationship with their parent.

Fathers who view the paternal caregiving role as important are more prepared for the fathering role and provide better quality of care, and therefore are more likely to have securely attached infants (Wong et al. 2009).

Attachment theory provides a framework for conceptualizing the nature and implications of parent-child relationships. According to the theory, children form ties to caregivers that vary in terms of the security of the bond. Children who form secure attachments are able to use the attachment figure as a safe haven in times of distress and as a secure base to support exploration and play at times of low distress. More secure attachments are thought to be a product, in part, of caregiving histories in which a child has received responsive and sensitive care from an attachment figure. A hallmark of secure attachment is open and relaxed communication between parent and child, particularly with regard to communications concerning the experience of positive and negative affect. Further, attachment has implications for functioning outside of the parent-child relationship in that more securely attached children are expected to demonstrate greater curiosity and confidence when working on challenging tasks and to have less difficulty in social interactions with familiar peers (Kerns et al. 2000).

● ● ●

Quality of Time

The quality of time that a father spends with his child is a significant factor in father-child attachment. Responsible fathering does not just consist of provision and economic support, but also has to include presence and actual involvement in the caring practices as well. Fathers who get involved in the practical chores on a day-to-day basis and do so with ongoing continuous awareness of the baby's state of mind also have better father-child attachment (Haavind 2011).

One country that acknowledges the importance of fathers' care and father-child attachment is Norway. Since 1993, Norway has increased paid parental leave for fathers from four to ten weeks. Norway believes and argues that men and women should have equal rights concerning economic compensation for childcare. Similarly, in Iceland, the paid leave for one year is divided into three, reserving one third for the mother, one third for the father, and one third for them to distribute as they please (Haavind 2011).

On the other hand, it has been significantly proved that fathers' work hours make unique contributions, in that fathers who work longer hours are less likely to have securely attached infants (Wong et al. 2009). It is possible that fathers who work longer hours may experience greater work-to-family spillover and therefore spend less quality time with their infants. It has been documented that fathers who report spending more time with their infants tend to have more positive interactions with their infants. As such, fathers who work longer hours may have fewer opportunities to foster their infants' attachment security (Wong et al. 2009).

A study of military parents also stressed the importance of spending quality time with their children regardless of any specific activity. Today's military comprises 1.2 million active-duty males, and almost 43 percent have dependent children (Willerton et al. 2011). Children's responses to deployment vary according to their developmental age, but they frequently include refusal to eat (infants), crying, poor sleep (toddlers), regression to earlier behaviors, clinginess, fearfulness (preschoolers), acting out, sleep disturbances, problems in school, isolation, rebellion, loss of interest in school or peers, and substance abuse (Willerton et al. 2011). Fathers reported age-appropriate activities such as reading stories, going to the park, reviewing homework, and getting children ready for school. In addition, fathers described attending school functions, teaching their children, playing sports and video games, and participating in their musicals and plays. Fathers especially enjoyed playing and rough-housing with their preschoolers and coaching sports with older children (Willerton et al. 2011).

An interesting factor highlighted in the examination of father-child quality of time spent was that fathers of boys spend more time with their children than fathers of girls, regardless of the age of the child. It was found that fathers feel better prepared to play or interact with a male infant with whom they share the same sex role identity. Fathers also are expected to have a greater role in raising sons than daughters (Rouyer et al. 2007). Also, according to the involvement index, which measures the amount and quality of the parent-child involvement relationship, fathers of boys are more involved with their child than fathers of girls, particularly in activities of caregiving. This is due to fathers perceiving themselves as having more important roles in the socialization of boys than girls. Another possibility is that fathers also feel less comfortable with the body of their daughters. On the other hand, fathers of girls feel that they need to protect their daughters more than their boys (Rouyer et al. 2007).

Findings in another study indicated that children did not feel connected to fathers where their fathers were not assimilated into the ebb and flow of everyday life and were not attuned to what was happening in their day-to-day lives, even when contact was regular. Children felt absent fathers generally were not available to hear about and react to the day-to-day events that happened in their lives. These children also reported negative relationships with fathers who were unreliable and frequently cancelled visitation arrangements (Nixon, Greene, and Hogan 2012).

It is widely acknowledged that it is the quality of time fathers and children spend together, rather than the quantity, that is important for children's development. Based on a meta-analysis of sixty-three studies, how often fathers see their children is less important than the fathers' engagement in authoritative parenting and the quality of the emotional ties that have formed between the father and child. Thus, regular father-child contact, while necessary, is not sufficient in and of itself to under-pin close father-child relationships (Nixon, Greene, and Hogan 2012).

However, it may be challenging for nonresi-dent fathers to engage in authoritative parenting when contact time is punctuated by gaps of days or even weeks and thus precludes involvement in a range of parenting tasks. A number of studies have reported that nonresident fathers are typically not involved in day-to-day activities such as homework, instead tending to be indulgent and permissive and to engage in leisure activities with their children to ensure that their children enjoy themselves during their limited time together (Nixon, Greene, and Hogan 2012).

• • •

Impact of Father-Mother Conflict on Attachment

Evidence suggests that the processes involved in the development of the infant-father attachment relationship may differ from those involved in the development of the infant-mother attachment rela-tionship. In particular, the quality of parental rela-tions has been suggested to have a greater impact on fathers' relationship with infants compared to that of mothers. Some researchers have proposed that fathers view marriage and fatherhood as one and the same, so the quality of different family relationships is more consistent for fathers than for mothers (Caldera and Lindsey 2006). A well-functioning coparenting system, characterized by parents' mutual support of each other's child-rearing behaviors, may contribute to children's concordant attachment to the mother and father by providing a consistent child-rearing environment (Caldera and Lindsey 2006).

There is a growing body of research demonstrating that multiple levels of family functioning are linked to the quality of parent-child attachment relationships. Whereas other researchers in this area have focused on marital functioning, these researchers extended this line of investigation to include the coparenting relationship. It was found that competitive coparenting was linked to parents' perception of a less secure parent-child attachment relationship. Thus, it appears that parents who vie with each other for their child's attention and work against one another when playing with their child may undermine their child's sense of confidence or security in his or her relationship with each parent (Caldera and Lindsey 2006).

Researchers also examined how the father-mother relationship impacted the father-child attachment bond. It was found that a couple who showed high psychological aggression in problem-solving interactions had children who were less securely attached to their fathers (Laurent, Kim, and Capaldi 2008). A history of aggressive partner interactions may have fostered longer-term hostility within the parents' relationship that detracted from sensitive or attuned parenting and emotional availability. These parents may also be less able to act as a secure base for children (Laurent, Kim, and Capaldi 2008). Overall, it has been found and demonstrated that couples' conflict and attachment characteristics have a greater effect on father-child attachment security than on mother-child security. It would appear that the child's developing relationship with the father is more vulnerable to difficulties in the parents' romantic relationship (Laurent, Kim, and Capaldi 2008).

Also, those children who have been sensitized to parental anger have been found to exhibit increased negativity, have negative expectations about marital relationships, show compromised physiological regulation, and have insecure attachment relationships with their parents. Marital conflict affects attachment indirectly because highly conflicted couples may be less emotionally available to adequately protect their infant, which leads the infant to develop a negative internal working model of the parent-child relationship. Also, marital conflict directly impacts the infant's overall feeling of security. That is because infants may feel uncomfortable or even frightened when they observe overt conflictual behavior in their attachment figures (Braungart-Rieker and Karrass 1999).

Another study reported evidence that children from families characterized by high levels of interparental conflict are rejected by their peers. According to emotional security theory, exposure to interparental conflict produces increased negative emotional arousal and feelings of interparental insecurity in children, leading directly to problems in peer relationships. Marital conflict may reduce parents' warmth and sensitivity in interactions with their children, thus disrupting the child's ability to form a secure emotional attachment with the parent, which has consequences for children's adjustment outside of the family (Lindsey, Caldera, and Tankersley 2009).

Attachment theorists suggest that in the process of forming an attachment bond to the parent, children develop an internal working model of relationships. Those children with a working model based on a secure attachment to their parent develop positive expectations of social partners, whereas children who have established a working model based on insecure attachment to their parent have difficulty trusting others and forming meaningful relationships. In this way, marital conflict may have an indirect effect on the quality of children's peer relationships through the parent-child attachment relationship (Lindsey, Caldera, and Tankersley 2009).

When looking at parental separation or divorce, children in joint custody were better adjusted than children in sole custody arrangements and were, in fact, as well adjusted as children whose parents remained married. Therefore, it would be ideal if divorced parents wishing to relocate could be persuaded to wait until their children were at least two or three years old, because the children would then be better equipped with the cognitive and language skills necessary to maintain long-distance relationships, particularly when formidable distances separate them from one of their parents (Kelly and Lamb 2003).

The extent and variety of communication between nonmoving parents and their distant children is crucial. Young children benefit from both auditory and visual reminders of their absent parent. Photographs and videos of nonmoving parents, along with their children, constitute the easiest way of refreshing children's memories. For children under the age of three, telephone contacts are often unsatisfying, at least to the absent parent, because children have limited language abilities and may be confused by disembodied human voices over the phone, but brief phone calls should still take place. Although some two-year-olds may occasionally become distressed when they recognize the voices of missed and loved parents, others may be cheered by hearing reassuring voices. To hold the toddlers' attention and institute reliable patterns, the calls should be brief but regular. Videos of young children and the parents with whom they have limited contact after relocation can help maintain attachments (Kelly and Lamb 2003).

Evidence has revealed that never-married biological fathers are at considerable risk for low levels of involvement with nonresident children. This includes fathers with children from other unions, as these fathers are at risk for decreased involvement with their new children. Dividing time between children living in separate residences may decrease involvement in comparison to fathers whose children live in the same household. Another group of non-married fathers are those fathers who do not establish legal paternity and who do not pay formal or informal child support, as these fathers are also at risk for low levels of father involvement. Lack of establishment of paternity is associated with reduced contact with the child and a lower frequency of overnight child visits. Research has also shown a significant association between child support payments and paternal involvement. It was estimated that improved child support enforcement resulted in a 45 percent increase in never-married fathers' visitation with their children (Fagan and Palkovitz 2007).

After parental separation or divorce, the mother's formation of a romantic relationship with a new male partner has been found to affect the likelihood of continued father involvement, which in turn impacts the father-child attachment bond (Gee and Rhodes 2003). This is due to fathers having conflicts with the mother and possibly with the mother's new partner. Due to these conflicts, many fathers are discouraged and tend to refrain from having contact with the mother, which in turn affects their frequency and level of contact with their child.

Overall, data have consistently shown that fathers who were involved during the pregnancy were more likely to stay engaged with their children throughout the early childhood years. These results suggest that the feelings and thoughts fathers have about their children before birth are linked to the quality of later parenting (Bouchard 2012). Prenatal programs could incorporate discussions on the importance of fathers' involvement during pregnancy and the varied ways future fathers can be connected to or involved with the fetus and their partners during the pregnancy (Bouchard 2012). Finally, the longer fathers are involved in their children's lives, the more likely it is that they will feel invested and, hence, remain involved even when the parents are no longer in a relationship (Cabrera et al. 2008).

● ● ●

Sensitivity and Its Impact on Attachment

Sensitivity is defined as the ability to perceive and interpret the signals and communications implicit in the infant's behavior and how a parent responds to them appropriately and promptly. It was found that higher levels of paternal sensitivity are associated with more infant-father attachment security. Examples of sensitivity include contingent vocalizations, encouragement of the child's efforts, and soothing the infant in times of distress. Traditionally, fathers have been described as focused on stimulating and exploratory play interactions with their children, with less emphasis on emotional support and warmth. Mothers might relate to their infants with sensitive warmth, whereas fathers might choose sensitive stimulation as a way to promote feelings of security in their infants. Stimulation can be described as any activating interaction on the part of the parent directed toward the infant in order to promote his or her exploration or playful behaviors. Examining determinants of the attachment relationship with the infant is important, since several studies have shown positive correlates with a secure father-child attachment relationship. For example, children with a secure attachment relationship with their father have fewer behavior problems and show higher levels of sociability (Lucassen et al. 2011).

In addition, sensitivity refers to a parent's ability to recognize and accurately interpret the child's signals and respond in ways that are affectionate, well timed, and appropriately stimulating. Sensitive parents are attuned to their child's needs and attend to those needs in a responsive and nonintrusive manner. In theoretical and empirical work on attachment, early sensitive parents are thought of as promoting children's emotional security and sense of trust in their caregiver (Brown, Mangelsdorf, and Neff 2012).

Also, sensitivity might moderate the relationship between father involvement and attachment security, in that secure attachment is most likely to occur when fathers are highly involved and highly sensitive. Having a child who is securely attached to them may increase fathers' motivation and self-confidence as parents, both of which are key determinants of sensitive and engaged fathering. Therefore, fathers with securely attached infants may go on to show greater involvement and sensitivity with their children in later childhood (Brown, Mangelsdorf, and Neff 2012).

• • •

Biological and Child-Development Concerns

Past researchers have found many implications of how insecure father-child attachment has impacted children's development. When looking at female biological development, it has been found that girls who grow up in homes without their biological fathers tend to go through puberty earlier than their peers. As specified by evolutionary causal theory, younger sisters had earlier menarche than their older sisters in biologically disrupted families, but not in biologically intact families. This data suggests that early exposure to disordered paternal behavior, followed by family disruption and residential separation from the father, can lead to substantially earlier menarche (Tither and Ellis 2008).

There are three competing classes of explanation for the observed relations between family disruption/father absence and earlier pubertal development: (1) Family disruption/father absence and associated factors may actually cause earlier pubertal development in daughters. (2) The relation between family disruption/father absence and earlier pubertal development in daughters may derive from a family-wide environmental confound. (3) The relation between family disruption/father absence and earlier pubertal development in daughters may derive from shared genetic confound (Tither and Ellis 2008).

1. Family disruption/father absence and associated factors may actually cause earlier pubertal development in daughters. One theoretical

camp has explicitly advanced this causal argument. Evolutionary-based models of development experience, such as psychosocial acceleration theory and paternal investment theory, posit that family disruption/father absence places daughters at risk for precocious sexual development and reproductive behavior. Paternal investment theory emphasizes that girls detect and internally encode information specifically about the quality of paternal investment in childhood as a basis for calibrating the development of (a) neurophysiologic systems involved in the timing of pubertal maturation and (b) related motivational systems, which make certain types of sexual behavior more or less likely in adolescence. An assumption of the theory is that early experiences provide assays of the quality of male-female relationships and the father's investment in the family. These assays in turn provide input to the regulatory mechanisms that control sexual development. Girls whose early family experiences are characterized by discordant male-female relationships and relatively low paternal investment register that male parental investment is not crucial

to reproduction. These girls are hypothesized to develop in a manner that speeds
rates of pubertal maturation, accelerates
onset of sexual activity, and orients the individual toward relatively unstable pair bonds.
Conversely, girls whose early family experiences are characterized by more harmoni-
ous male-female relationships and relatively
high paternal investment are hypothesized
to develop in the opposite manner. Either
way, the girl entrains a developmental tra-
jectory that, in the adult social environment
into which she will mature, was likely to
have promoted reproductive success during human evolutionary history (Tither and
Ellis 2008).

2. The relation between family disruption/father
absence and earlier pubertal development
in daughters may derive from a family-wide
environmental confound. Family-wide environmental effects are causal factors that differ
among families but are shared within families.
A family-wide environmental confound could
cause both family disruption/father absence
and earlier pubertal development. For example, poverty is associated with both elevated

rates of family disruption/father absence and, according to recent studies in the United States, earlier pubertal development in girls. If poverty is the underlying cause of the relation between family disruption/father absence and earlier pubertal development, then the "effect" of family disruption/father absence is in fact spurious (Tither and Ellis 2008).

3. The relation between family disruption/father absence and earlier pubertal development in daughters may derive from a shared genetic confound. Behavior geneticists refer to this type of association as a gene-environment correlation. Specifically, girls who mature earlier tend to exhibit earlier onset of sexual activity and earlier age at first marriage and first birth. This covariation may occur because early pubertal timing results in precocious sexual and reproductive behavior or because pubertal, sexual, and reproductive timing are genetically correlated traits. Early reproduction in turn is associated with increased probability of divorce and lower quality paternal investment. Because mothers who mature early tend to have daughters who are mature

early, the correlation between family disruption and timing of pubertal maturation in girls may be spurious; that is, it may simply be due to genetic transmission of pubertal timing and associated behavioral characteristics. This non-causal explanation converges with molecular genetic research demonstrating the effects of allelic variations on pubertal timing (Tither and Ellis 2008).

In disrupted families in which sisters were exposed to serious paternal dysfunction, the younger sisters had substantially advanced menarche. Indeed, these younger sisters attained menarche almost a year earlier than did younger sisters from other families who experienced comparable amounts of family disruption/father absence but were not exposed to serious paternal dysfunction. Also, their older sisters who experienced less father absence but had more prolonged exposure to serious paternal dysfunction also experienced advanced menarche. Thus, early exposure to serious paternal dysfunction, followed by family disruption and departure of the biological father from the home, contributed to earlier attainment of menarche. This conclusion is based on genetically and environmentally controlled within-family sibling data, as well as between-family comparisons. It should be noted that the effect size for the within-family analysis was about twice as large as that for the between-family analysis, indicating that the effect was primarily driven by direct comparisons between older and younger sisters (Tither and Ellis 2008).

It was further found that early father-absent girls were almost three times more likely than father-present girls to have experienced menarche before age twelve. Also, early father-absent girls were found to be almost twice as likely as father-present girls to have completed pubertal development by the seventh grade (Ellis 2004). Paternal investment theory provides the foundation for a series of predictions about the role for fathers and other men in the regulation of girls' pubertal timing. Although the theory began with a focus on father absence versus presence, it has since been elaborated to include multiple dimensions of paternal investment and specifically conceptualizes father effects as distinct from the more general effects of familial and ecological stressors. Paternal investment theory has now been tested in a number of investigations and has received provisional empirical support. In well-nourished populations, girls from father-absent homes tend to experience earlier pubertal development than do girls from father-present homes, and the earlier father absence occurs, the greater the effect. There is also initial longitudinal evidence that within father-present homes, higher levels of paternal care-taking and involvement are associated with later pubertal development in daughters. Finally, there is consistent evidence that quality of paternal invest-ment uniquely predicts timing of pubertal develop-ment in daughters independently of other aspects of the family ecology (Ellis 2004).

Also, it was noted by an extensive body of research in Western societies that early maturation in girls was associated with a variety of negative health and psycho-social outcomes, including mood disorders, substance abuse, adolescent pregnancy, and a variety of cancers of the reproductive system. Given these links, it is critical to understand the life experiences and path-ways that place girls at increased risk for early puber-tal maturation. This understanding would have great relevance to the long-term goal of informing early intervention-prevention strategies. Many correlational studies have identified biological family disruption/ father absence as a risk factor for early pubertal devel-opment in daughters. Moreover, the earlier that family disruption/father absence occurs, the earlier daughters tend to experience puberty (Tither and Ellis 2008).

When female sexual activity was researched, it was reported that paternal involvement during childhood was related to delayed menarche and ages of first sexual intercourse and first childbirth. One area of research that has successfully used life-history theory is the study of the relationship between family environment and pubertal timing. Having a more supportive family, especially a warm relationship with the father, is related to later onset of menarche in girls (Vigil and Geary 2006). Female participants in previous sexual activity studies reported that paternal involvement led them to delay their first sexual activity and reproduction or childbirth. One of the positive functions of father-daughter involvement in the daughter's reproduction is that delayed reproduction provides the daughter with added social competitiveness before competing for mates and will increase her ability to invest in her own children during adulthood. Also, delayed childbirth for daughters was associated with higher levels of parental income, education, and investment in higher adult social status (Vigil and Geary 2006).

Father involvement and father-child secure attachment has been associated with decreased danger of the child's injury risk. Past studies have found that the role of a father who resided in or out of the home had an impact on a child's subsequent injury risk. Results found that children who experienced fathers in their biological home during toddlerhood experienced lower rates of subsequent injuries than children who experienced the departure of their father from their home (Schwebel and Brezausek 2007). Unintentional injury is the leading cause of death in American children ages one to eighteen, killing more children than the next twenty causes of death combined. Unintentional injuries are typically not accidental but rather are caused by a range of psychosocial and environmental factors. One of the strongest risk factors for pediatric injury, especially among young children, is the lack of supervision. It was found that the addition of a second adult to the household serves to protect children from risk, while the loss of an adult increases injury risk (Schwebel and Brezausek 2007). Therefore, results suggest that father transitions in a child's household during the toddler years are related to that child's subsequent risk for injury. This effect was maintained even after including a wide range of child, parent, and family characteristics in multivariate models (Schwebel and Brezausek 2007).

Research has also found that paternal investment does lower infant and child mortality risks in many contexts. Father absence at any point prior to the child's fifteenth birthday was associated with a mortality rate of more than 45 percent, as compared with a mortality rate of 20 percent for children whose father resides with them until their fifteenth birthday (Geary 2000).

Father involvement in the health and health care of their children is considered an important priority for two primary reasons. First, there is an inextricable link between parental child-rearing practices and the health and well-being of children, which is highlighted in the extant literature detailing with both the positive and negative child outcomes associated with father involvement across the child's life span. Second, parental child-rearing practices can affect the health of parents, with preliminary research indicating that involvement with children can have both positive and negative effects on the father's health and well-being. For example, for preterm infants, father involvement was positively associated with cognitive development within African-American families. Three-year-old children benefited from father involvement with more advanced language development. Other interesting medical findings in past research include positive associations found between father involvement and the cognitive development of children with Down syndrome, as well as with treatment adherence and the quality of life among adolescents with a chronic disease (Garfield and Isacco 2012).

Empirical research has suggested that insecure attachment is linked with more frequent symptoms of pain and poor health. Insecure attachment is also linked to anxiety, psychosomatic illness, and physical complaints in both adolescents and adults. Several studies found that some styles of insecure attachment were associated with poorer glycemic control and poorer adherence to blood glucose testing and injections (Rosenberg and Shields 2009). Poor father-child attachment has been known to establish enduring dysregulations in the child's physiological stress response, promoting pathophysiology in the brain and body and contributing to hypertension, heart disease, infectious disease, and other illnesses. Furthermore, poor father-child relationships and more distress were both associated with poorer reported physical health as young adults (Fabricius and Luecken 2007).

Finally, it has been found that the quality of family dynamics and father-child attachment are related to the timing of developmental milestones such as menarche, sexuality, adult attachment styles, social cognitions, and reproductive trajectories. Girls with high-investing fathers at home begin dating and initiate sex at a later age. Girls in father-absent homes are more likely to have internalizing disorders, whereas boys in father-absent homes are more likely to have externalizing disorders and be less popular. These studies have found that the nature and quality of father-child interactions have a long-lasting impact on the response to psychosocial stressors and development (Byrd-Craven et al. 2012).

• • •

Academic and Educational Achievement

It has been found that children with secure father-child attachment and father involvement also have greater academic achievement than children with insecure father-child attachment or no father involvement. Educational attainment is one of the best predictors of occupational and income level in adulthood and is linked to a number of other outcomes, including mental and physical health. Educational achievement is also preventative intervention aimed at improving psychosocial outcomes. Positive academic and social behaviors predict fewer behavioral problems, less involvement with deviant peers, less likelihood of drug and alcohol abuse, and better educational attainment in adulthood (Pears et al. 2012).

Some other benefits found in academic achievement in children with secure father-child attachment are better social performance in school and lower rates of school suspensions or behavioral referrals. In children from low socioeconomic status, father involvement was found to be a protective factor in family instability and academic achievement. Positive father-child secure attachment also has been found to promote school readiness and school adjustment in children. It was found that positive parenting of children in kindergarten was an indicator of higher grades in high school (Pears et al. 2012). Further, it was found that father involvement was specifically associated with cognitive gains and higher achievement in math and reading. Also, teachers reported that children with father involvement tended to be less demanding of their teachers for attention, less defiant and uncooperative, and engaged in more prosocial behaviors than children who did not have regular contact with their fathers (Howard et al. 2006).

Children whose fathers used more positive early parental control had higher Performance IQ scores later in development than other children. Research also suggests that fathers enhance their children's cognitive functioning through play. Perhaps fathers who demonstrate the positive use of parental control during play strengthen nonverbal abilities. The effects of paternal control on children's nonverbal cognitive functioning was statistically significant over a span of six to ten years and accounted for more variance in Performance IQ scores than any other predictor, even when "baseline" IQ at pre-school age was controlled (Pougnet et al. 2011).

An interesting study conducted on the degree to which popular child-rearing books reflect a new image of fatherhood found that most children's books are written primarily for mothers. In a sample of twenty-three child-rearing books with 56,379 paragraphs, only 2,363 paragraphs (4.2 percent) referenced fathers. The image of a traditional family has changed in the last thirty years. It is estimated that 16 percent of families fit into the traditional model of gender-role differentiation where the father is the wage earner and the mother is responsible for homemaking and child rearing. Popular child-rearing books do not seem to emphasize the importance of fathers' roles. In a comparison of illustrations and parent gender images, of 450 images that portrayed adults with children, females were portrayed in 311 images (69.1 percent) whereas males were depicted in 103 images (22.9 percent). In 36 images (8.0 percent), both males and females were represented. This investigation suggests that child-rearing books are written largely for a female audience and that fathers' roles are peripheral and limited (Fleming and Tobin 2005). This points to a societal influence that does not allow for positive paternal story-telling or highlighting the importance of the father-child relationship. More literature that can highlight and show the important role of father-child relationship is needed.

Therefore, it is important to note that one of the strongest influences of fathers is related to school success. Effects include less defiance, greater cooperation with teachers, higher cognitive functioning, higher grades in math and reading, and school readiness.

● ● ●

Emotional and Psychological Functioning

Research has indicated that children who experience fathers' absence from the home at various points during childhood are more likely than other children to display internalizing problems, such as sadness, social withdrawal, and anxiety, as well as externalizing problems, such as aggression, impulsivity, and hyperactivity. Another study conducted in the United States found that children with absent fathers displayed more antisocial behaviors than children with their father in the home (Pougnet et al. 2011).

One of the emotional and psychological effects on children with insecure father-child attachment or no father involvement is separation anxiety disorder (SAD). Separation anxiety disorder is characterized by non-age-appropriate, excessive worry and anxiety regarding separation from caregivers or from the home. Paternal absence was found to have an important influence on vulnerability to SAD. Symptoms include extreme distress when separating from attachment figures and chronic worrying about losing or being separated from such figures. Additionally, children may refuse to go to school or sleep alone, demonstrate fear of being away from attachment figures in the home, have nightmares about separation, and complain of physical symptoms in anticipation of separation. The key features of this disorder are the non-age-appropriate and excessive nature of the symptoms. For instance, a fear of being away from caregivers may be age-appropriate for a small child but becomes problematic when the child is school-aged and refuses to go to school because of excessive anxiety about separation from caregivers. It was also found that children who suffered from SAD were significantly associated with adult anxiety disorder, including panic disorder and phobias (Cronk et al. 2004).

Also, it has been found that fathers are more likely to serve as playmates, which can be important for developing healthy social and emotional skills in their children. A secure attachment to the father may enhance opportunities for children to establish secure attachment relationships and social and emotion-regulation skills (Kerns et al. 2000).

An interesting finding showed there was a direct connection between attachment and body image dissatisfaction in college women. Attachment anxiety corresponds to an underlying negative working model of self and involves low self-esteem and chronic fears of abandonment in close relationships. Women with this latter form of adult attachment insecurity may be especially vulnerable to fears of being negatively evaluated with regard to how their partners view their physical attractiveness. This emphasizes that high-quality parental bonds and adult attachment security help women resist the negative influence of media portrayals by not internalizing the images, thereby experiencing greater satisfaction with their body image. Therapists working with clients presenting problems with body image dissatisfaction would benefit from assessing the client's attachment history, current attachment style, and preference about attending media sources. Counselors might be able to decrease body image concerns directly by helping women reduce their exposure to harmful media images and develop effective cognitive strategies that prevent internalizing the images that their clients do see (Cheng and Mallinckrodt 2009).

Research found that a nondepressed father could buffer his child from the most severe consequences of a depressed mother. Several studies show that children whose mother is depressed are at a greatly elevated risk of both internalizing and externalizing behavior problems. However, that risk is substantially reduced or even eliminated if the child has a coresident father who is not depressed. Also, if a child fails to receive adequate maternal support, the support received from a father may take on added importance because of its compensatory value (Martin, Ryan, and Brooks-Gunn 2010). The importance of secure father-child attachment can have lasting effects well into adulthood.

Substantial research suggests that emotional adjustment in adults is associated with memories of emotional bonds with parents. For example, adults who recalled their parents as cold and emotionally unexpressive were likely to have high levels of depression. Contemporary theorists explain these findings in terms of damaged and incomplete sense of self that results when parents are not sufficiently emotionally responsive. This also suggests that young adults who recall poor-quality emotional bonds with parents have developed a negative self-concept (Cheng and Mallinckrodt 2009).

On the other hand, fathers' depressive symptoms were directly related to children's internalizing problems. Studies that have examined the role of emotional security and the influence of fathers on their children's adjustment came to the conclusion that fathers' depression directly affects their children's emotional and psychological health. In terms of fatherhood depression, a relation was also found between dysphoria, paternal marital conflict, child emotional security, and child adjustment. Fathers experiencing stress and dissatisfaction in their marital relationships may be less loving and attentive to the needs of their children or offer less emotional support and positive stimulation, which may be associated with adjustment problems in children (Schacht, Cummings, and Davies 2009).

In relation to fathers and children's emotional security in the family, emotional security theory posit that children appraise family situations in relation to their own security about their family's and personal well-being with the goal of preserving their own sense of protection and security within the family. Therefore, in the presence of marital conflict or other family dysfunction linked with fathers, emotional insecurity may be associated with increased adjustment problems in children. Children's emotional security about family relationships has been linked with risk for internalizing, and less consistently, externalizing, problems (Schacht, Cummings, and Davies 2009).

When children have lost a parent due to separation or death, this will lead to some serious implications for those children. Research has shown that children who have lost their parent have long-term psychological reactions and serious problems. A common consequence of a child losing a parent is that this child will suffer from depression (Zvizdic and Butollo 2000). Children show some difficulties in psychosocial adjustment if they have been separated from family members very close to them, or if they know nothing about them. These difficulties in adjustment can provoke various psychological problems. It has been found that if a high degree of ambiguity exists over a long time, school-aged children and adolescents run the risk of maladaptation. According to theories of self-formation and the development of self-concepts, we can expect that self-processes will be particularly weakened through missing relatives. In a grief study, it was found that grieving adolescents show characteristics of depressive symptoms, even two months after the loss. These children also experience lack of interest in activities that they previously enjoyed, and a high percentage of suicidal wishes (Zvizdic and Butollo 2000).

Substance abuse was also found to be an implication of insecure father-child attachment or lack of father involvement. A study found that not having been raised with a biological father present was associated with significantly increased odds of alcohol abuse. Father absence was a more important risk factor for rural young offenders, but school dropout was associated with more hazardous drinking among young offenders in urban areas. Family composition is strongly related to adolescent alcohol abuse. Adolescents who live in single-parent families, or without any biological parents, drink alcohol more frequently and at more dangerous levels than adolescents who live in two-parent families. Two-parent families provide protection against substance abuse through improved supervision. Supervision of young people reduces the interaction with deviant peers and hence reduces exposure to substance use. Research also suggests a gender difference. Having both parents present and providing adequate supervision benefits both boys and girls. However, girls living in single-mother families are more likely to drink at a high-risk level than boys living in single-mother families (Kenny and Schreiner 2009).

Secure father-child attachment has many psychological and emotional effects on children. It is important to note to mental health treatment providers that one of the most obvious implications in many research findings is the importance of fathers in the treatment of their child's psychological, emotional, and adjustment difficulties (Jia, Kotila, and Schoppe-Sullivan 2012). Specifically, researchers found that fathering was more important for daughters' depression as well as behavioral and externalizing problems in sons (Day and Padilla-Walker 2009).

Fathers are unlikely to seek out treatment if doing so requires acknowledgment of a skill deficit.

Therefore, calling an intervention "parent train-ing" may discourage father participation, because the title implies a skills deficit. Framing behavior parenting training as a means of enhancing existing skill areas and using a less pejorative label might be better received by fathers. Also, changing the treat-ment setting from a classroom/didactic setting to one that includes an activity-oriented setting might make regular attendance at treatment reinforcing and relevant and promote the practice of parent-ing skills (Fabiano 2007). So mental health provid-ers will need to be creative in order to get fathers to participate in treatment for their child and for themselves.

• • •

Legal and Delinquency Concerns

There were also significant correlations found between insecure father-child attachment or lack of father involvement and issues of delinquency and illegal behaviors with these children and adolescents. Parental bonding was found to be related to several indicators of distress among incarcerated adoles-cents. For both males and females, hopelessness was found to be significantly associated with bonding style with the opposite-sex parent (McGarvey et al. 1999).

During early adolescence, excessive emotional separation from parents often leads to antisocial conduct, in part because it pushes children into contact with deviant peers (Hodges, Finnegan, and Perry 1999). Another interesting finding on anti-social behavior is the association between a father's incarceration and the child's higher risk of antiso-cial behavior. A specific association with children's antisocial propensity and the stressful experiences was caused by a parental incarceration. Social mod-eling processes point out that children who grow up seeing their parents respond to stressful life events with antisocial behavior may be socialized into hav-ing antisocial reactions to disruptive events, such as parental incarceration. It is clear that children with incarcerated parents are at increased risk for antiso-cial behavior compared with their peers (Murray, Farrington, and Sekol 2012).

On the other hand, men who are incarcerated also face many issues such as increased negative mental health, strained identity concerns, strained family relationships, and lack of community con-nections. The impact of incarceration has far-reach-ing consequences for men's functioning, including their mental and physical health as well as reintegration into the community. Identifying factors that influence men's functioning while in prison and upon release has a number of implications for these men, their families, and communities (Gordon et al. 2013).

In correctional facilities, men lose a sense of autonomy, familial support, and material goods, which are important components of men's identities. Given that environment and experiences help shape identity, incarceration may strip away or cause a flux in identity. According to the identity accumulation hypothesis, the greater the loss of multiple identities is, the more psychological distress is experienced (Iwamoto et al. 2012).

Therefore, if correctional facilities can continue to support programs that teach men about the importance of fathering, positive father-child attachment and relationships and encourage opportunities for these men to maintain a connection with their child, this could go a long way to allowing for these men to continue their relationship with their children upon their release from these correctional facilities.

• • •

Cultural Implications

Although fathering is considered critically important for understanding child socialization, father-child interactions across societies have been observed in very few studies (Feldman and Masalha 2010). Therefore, this book highlights some cultural implications that have been found to influence father-child secure attachment.

Although the importance of fathers has been established, the majority of research on fathering is based on data from middle-class European American families, and research on ethnic minority fathers, especially Latino fathers, has lagged significantly behind. This is a shortcoming in this area of study, as Latinos are the largest ethnic minority group in the United States, making up 16 percent of the population, and this number is expected to rise to 30 percent by the year 2050. Also, it has been found that Latino fathers are involved in some aspects of childcare to the same or possibly a greater extent as that of their European American counterparts (Cruz et al. 2011).

Studies of African American father-daughter relationships have indicated that daughters whose fathers were absent and who experienced alienation and disengagement in their relationship with their father were more likely to also experience symptoms of depression and problem behaviors at school (Pougnet et al. 2011).

In examining incarceration numbers of men, it was found that African American men make up 45 percent of the US prison population and are incarcerated at a rate that is eight times more than that of white men. The disparities in incarceration rates also amplify and perpetuate the problems faced by African American men, their families, and their community. The disproportionate number of incarcerated African American men makes it important to examine the effects of prison on their individual, family, and community functioning. African American men released from prison have identified difficulties securing stable living arrangements after incarceration, which negatively affects their ability to operate in society. Therefore, prison can interfere with African American men's family and other social networks and can diminish social cohesion (Gordon et al. 2013). This is a concern for African American men's ability to become positive fathers for their children.

It was noted that white children are more likely to receive child support and may see their fathers more often than minority children, whose fathers may be unemployed and have lower levels of education. But when fathers' financial contributions includes informal types of support, such as gifts or extra cash, minority nonresident fathers contribute at levels close to, or equal to, those of their white counterparts, suggesting that minority fathers may also visit children as frequently as white nonresident fathers. Also, minority nonresident fathers are more likely to maintain a romantic relationship with the child's mother than white fathers, which is linked to father involvement (Cabrera et al. 2008).

• • •

Chapter 3

• • •

Looking at Past Research and Findings

"Every dad, if he takes time out of his busy life to reflect upon his fatherhood, can learn ways to become an even better dad."

—*Jack Baker*

Arbona and Power (2003), a study on the relation of father attachment to self-esteem and self-reported involvement in antisocial behaviors, provides a view of the correlations between the attachment, self-esteem, and antisocial behavior measures by ethnic group for the validation and analysis sample. The study revealed that with one exception, the correlations between the mother and father attachment variables and self-esteem and anti-social behaviors were moderate, ranging from .14 to .42. The correlation of father avoidance and self-reported involvement in antisocial behaviors was not statistically significant for African-Americans. As expected, mother and father avoidance and anxiety scores were negatively related to self-esteem and positively related to self-reported involvement in antisocial behaviors (Arbona and Power 2003).

Ganiban et al. (2011), a study on understanding child-based effects on parenting, examined the degree to which a child's temperament moderates genetics and environmental contributions to parenting. When looking at child temperament and father negativity, analyses indicated that child negative emotionality moderated genetic and nonshared environmental contributions to father negativity. Also, it was found that there was greater variance in father negativity at higher levels of child negative emotionality. This change was accounted for by increased genetic and nonshared environmental contributions. Within the context of low child negative emotionality, most variance in fathers' negativity was explained by shared environmental factors. However, at higher levels of negative emotionality, genetic and shared environmental factors accounted for more variance than shared environmental factors (Ganiban et al. 2011).

When children demonstrated high degrees of shyness, variance in father negativity was primarily explained by nonshared environmental factors, and genetic factors accounted for little variance. However, when children demonstrated low levels of shyness, variance in father negativity was primarily explained by genetic factors, and nonshared environmental contributions were small. When children demonstrated lower levels of sociability, genetic contributions to father negativity were at their lowest, whereas shared environmental contributions were at their highest and explained most variance. Conversely, at higher levels of sociability, genetic factors accounted for most variance in father negativity, whereas shared environmental factors accounted for the least amount of variance (Ganiban et al. 2011).

Pougnet et al. (2011) studied the influence of fathers on their children's cognitive and behavioral functioning. In the study they were able to show the interaction between fathers' presence in middle childhood and paternal attainment in their preadolescence in predicting later performance IQ scores in their children's preadolescence. Even fathers with low paternal education will increase their children's IQ scores from 93 to 101 just by being present in their child's life. Fathers with high paternal education will have a similar impact on their children's IQ scores. Therefore, a father's level of education and his presence have been shown to have an effect on the children's IQ average. In summary, children whose fathers displayed more positive early parental control had higher performance IQ scores than other children after controlling for family and socioeconomic factors. In addition, fathers' presence predicted higher performance IQ score for fathers with fewer years of educational attainment (Pougnet et al. 2011).

Day and Padilla-Walker (2009) examined connectedness between externalizing behaviors and the child's age, gender, and self-regulation. These externalizing behaviors accounted for a statistically significant proportion of variance, with age positively related and gender and self-regulation negatively related to externalizing behaviors. No other steps resulted in a significant increase in variance. In analyzing for involvement, mother and father involvement produced a .02 increase in the proportion of variance accounted for father involvement that was negatively related to externalizing behaviors.

Thus, it can be concluded that fathers' involvement was significantly related to children's externalizing behaviors, and mothers' involvement was not. However, no conclusion can be made that fathering mattered more than mothering in this regard (Day and Padilla-Walker 2009).

When examining internalizing behaviors for connectedness in the adolescent's age and gender, while self-regulation accounted for a statistically significant proportion of variance, with self-regulation negatively related to internalizing behaviors. Mother and father connectedness produced a .02 increase in the proportion of variance accounted for father connectedness negatively related to internalizing behaviors. It was therefore determined that the coefficient for fathers was significantly larger than the coefficient for mothers. This suggests that fathering matters more than mothering in this regard (Day and Padilla-Walker 2009). In summary, this confirms that both mothers and fathers are significant; however, mothering is more consistently related to adolescents' problem behaviors. Fathers' parenting is more focused on norm compliance. A key finding in the study is that parental connectedness and involvement in the lives of their children is important, with fathering being more important for internalizing behaviors (Day and Padilla-Walker 2009).

Howard et al. (2006) found that children with greater levels of father contact had fewer behavioral problems and had higher scores on reading achievement. Although neither father contact nor maternal risk showed significant main effects, the interaction effect was significant, suggesting that the effect of father contact on children's internalizing behaviors was greater than those who had limited father contact. In contrast, for children with low-risk mothers, father contact was not associated with internalizing behaviors. It is important to note that 36.8 percent of children in the high-risk mother, limited father contact group were in the borderline and clinical range for internalizing, whereas only 16 percent would be expected in the population. In contrast, only 24.1 percent of children with father contact and low-risk mothers demonstrated elevated levels of internalizing behaviors at eight years. The study also found that at ten years old, children with greater father contact continued to show better socioemotional adjustment in academic contexts. It also revealed that children with limited father contact were more excitable and impulsive and more likely to disturb other children in class. Also, they were more quarrelsome and destructive than children who had higher levels of father contact. In addition, children with father contact were less likely to make excessive demands of their teachers' attention and were more cooperative in class than children who had lower levels of contact (Howard et al. 2006).

Father Hunger is defined as the emotional and psychological longing that a person has for a father who has been physically, emotionally, or psychologically distant in the person's life. Father hunger can develop at any point across the life span, although it may be most likely to develop if a person's father is somehow unavailable during childhood or adolescence. The participants of this study were students from two undergraduate psychology courses at a large, public, southeastern university. These students volunteered during an in-class administration and received extra credit. Of the 105 participants, 71 percent were women, and 29 percent were men. Ninety-three percent of the sample were between the ages of eighteen and twenty-two, and 71 percent were white/non-Hispanic, 16 percent Hispanic, 4 percent Asian American, 3 percent African American, and 6 percent other (Perrin et al. 2009).

From the two studies that were completed, the top three questionnaire items in Study 1 were "I couldn't get close enough to my dad in the time we had together," "It was hard to get my dad to really love me," and "I was jealous of other's relationships with their father." In Study 2, the top three questionnaire items were "It was hard to get my dad to really love me," "I wished that my dad found me as interesting as he did other people and things," and "I was jealous of others' relationships with their fathers." Other notable findings were "My father broke promises to me," "I remember doing special things for my dad and he did not fully appreciate them," and "My father never thought I was good enough" (Perrin et al. 2009).

Schwebel and Brezausek (2007), a study on the father transition in the household and young children's injury risk, discussed the mean number of injuries, both overall and in specific locations, for each of the four groups, as reported between the thirty-six-month assessment and the spring of the first grade. The highest rates of injuries tended to be among the children for whom a father left the home (0.67) and when the father was absent from the home (0.61). The lowest injury rate tended to be among the children who experienced the entry of a father in the home (0.26) during infancy or toddlerhood. The stable households, when the father remained present or remained absent, fell in the middle. The overall injury rate was significantly different across the four groups, and post hoc analyses indicated that the group for whom a father entered the home during toddlerhood had a significantly lower rate of injuries during the preschool and early school years compared to the other three groups (Schwebel and Brezausek 2007).

Howard et al. (2006) discussed how contact or no contact with a father had implications with the academic functioning of a child. The first item discussed was teacher's reports of how externalizing and internalizing behaviors are displayed with children. It was found that eight-year-old children with no contact with their fathers had a higher rate (60.41) of externalizing behaviors than children who had contact with their father (53.90). Children with contact with their fathers achieved higher math scores (88.27) than children without contact with their fathers (83.56). Also, eight-year-old children who had contact with their father had a better reading achievement rate (89.25) than children with no contact with their father (85.56) (Howard et al. 2006, 472).

Murray, Farrington, and Sekol (2012) looked at children's antisocial behavior, mental health, drug use, and educational performance after parental incarceration. This study found associations between parental incarceration and children's antisocial behavior, poor mental health, drug use, and low educational performance in all samples with relevant results. Across all samples, the pooled odds ratio for the association between parental incarceration and children's antisocial behavior was significant and fairly large. For poor mental health, the pooled odds ratio was non-significant across all samples and showed almost zero association with parental incarceration. Also, there was almost no association between parental incarceration and children's drug use. Parental incarceration was significantly associated with poor educational performance (Murray, Farrington, and Sekol 2012).

Chapter 4

● ● ●

Analysis and Evaluation of the Findings

"My father didn't tell me how to live.
He lived and let me watch him do it."

——CLARENCE BUDINGTON KELLAND

According to Arbona and Power (2003), father attachment is very important in assessing a child's self-esteem and antisocial behaviors within ethnic groups. Children without positive father attachment are at greater risk for low self-esteem and antisocial behaviors. This population of children is also at risk of delinquent behaviors and illegal activity and of experiencing anxiety disorders.

Ganiban et al. (2011) looked at the child's temperament and negative father behaviors. This highlights the emotional impact on children. For example, there was greater variance in father negativity at higher levels of child negative emotionality. When the father's negativity was high, the children had a higher negative emotional impact. Also, children who experienced a high degree of shyness were associated with high levels of father negativity. The impacts of genetics and environment are also noted concerns. Genetics factors accounted for most variance in father negativity, whereas shared environmental factors accounted for the least amount of variance.

Pougnet et al. (2011) found that even fathers with low educational levels can still have an impact by being present and having a positive relationship with their children. They also found that children without a relationship with their father had an average IQ of 93, but when the father was present, children had an average IQ of 101, which is very remarkable. This can be due to the father's influence on the importance and follow-up regarding their child's academic and educational process.

Day and Padilla-Walker (2009) looked again at the importance of father-child attachment in the impact of externalizing and internalizing behaviors. When fathers have a healthy attachment with their children, their children will be experience a lower level of externalizing and internalizing behavioral and emotional concerns. They showed how fathering has more implications to internal and external behavioral concerns in their children.

Howard et al. (2006) illustrated the effect of father contact on children's internalizing behaviors as a function of maternal risk. It was noted that 36.8 percent of children in the high-risk mother, limited father contact group were in the borderline and clinical range for internalizing, whereas only 16 percent would be expected in the population. In contrast, only 24.1 percent of children with father contact and low-risk mothers demonstrated elevated levels of internalizing behaviors at eight years of age. Once again, this highlights the importance of child-father attachment in the risk of internalizing behavioral concerns.

Perrin et al. (2009) highlighted a lot of emotional and psychological feelings that individuals had in relation to father hunger. Father hunger is defined as the emotional and psychological longing that a person has for a father who has been physically, emotionally, or psychologically distant in the person's life. Therefore, many children and adults who do not have a positive child-father attachment still long for a positive child-father relationship. This father hunger can be a risk factor for many of the emotional, psychological, academic, legal, and cultural concerns that many of these individuals can suffer from due to not having a relationship with their father.

Schwebel and Brezausek (2007) highlighted the physical impacts of injuries to children who do not have a father present in the home. These children are at a higher risk of physical injuries. This is because there is a higher risk of low supervision when the father is not in the home and the mother is the primary caretaker and has the sole responsibility of supervision of the child. Even though there may be a stepparent in the home for a second parent for supervision, the rate of children being injured in the home is still a factor and concern.

Howard et al. (2006) displayed very easily how many areas of eight- and ten-year-old children can be affected when a father is present and when the father is not present. Areas such as external and internal behaviors, math and reading achievement, and hyperactivity and conduct problems are affected. In addition, some other problems are demanding the teacher's attention, excitable and impulsive behaviors, disturbing other children in the classroom, defiance, fearfulness, and quarrelsome and destructive behaviors. Children with no father contact have greater problems with the abovementioned behavioral and academic performance.

Murray, Farrington, and Sekol (2012) showed the associations between parental incarceration and children's antisocial behavior, poor mental health, drug use, and low educational performance in all samples with relevant results. Many researchers have highlighted the negative impact of parental incarceration on their children. It was interesting to see that according to this one study, there was almost no association between parental incarceration and children's drug use. Could it be that drug use in children can be caused by no contact with their father and not just by parental incarceration? On the other hand, parental incarceration was significantly associated with poor educational performance in children.

• • •

Questions to Be Answered in Regard to Impacts of Fatherhood

The primary questions to be assessed in this book are as follows: How does a lack of father-child attachment affect child development? How does a lack of father-child attachment affect a child's academic achievement? How does a lack of father-child attachment affect emotional and psychological functioning? Lastly, how is a lack of father-child attachment a risk factor for legal or delinquency issues?

With the research presented in this book, the above questions can be answered as follows. A lack of father-child attachment does affect a child's development, emotional functioning, and psychological functioning. We have seen how a lack of father-child attachment has negative impacts and higher risk of emotional and psychological functioning of these children and individuals. We have seen how these children with a lack of father-child attachment will have higher external and internal behavioral concerns, suffer from low self-esteem, have a higher degree of anxiety and depression, and have other emotional concerns.

A lack of father-child attachment does affect a child's academic functioning. We have seen how children without a father-child attachment will have lower IQ scores, lower math and reading achievement levels, and multiple classroom behavioral concerns such as requiring more of the teacher's attention and disruptive behaviors in the classroom.

Also, the research and journal articles have discussed how children with a lack of father-child attachment can be at a higher risk for legal and delinquency issues. Children with no father-child attachment are at higher risk for externalizing behaviors that can lead to delinquency and legal issues. Not only do these children suffer from poor social skills, but also these children can then interact with other children with similar poor social skills and disruptive behaviors that can lead to delinquency and legal concerns. During early adolescence, excessive emotional separation from parents often leads to antisocial conduct, in part because it pushes children into contact with deviant peers (Hodges, Finnegan, and Perry 1999).

● ● ●

Summary of Findings

The purpose of this book is to review the past and current literature on secure attachment that discussed the father-child attachment. This book has highlighted the importance of father-child attachment, the importance of father involvement, and the positive and negative impacts on child development. There are major trends and interests of father-child attachment within the field of psychology and child development. This book reviewed the impacts of father-child attachment on child development, academic achievement, emotional and psychological functioning in children, and legal and delinquency issues among children who do not have a secure father-child attachment.

I was able to support the importance and clinical significance of Bowlby's attachment theory. Bowlby's attachment theory highlights that the adaptive patterns of parent-child interaction in the early years promote the development of secure relationships between children and their caregivers. Therefore, this early relationship can serve as a source of emotional security that promotes healthy functioning across many domains of development (Brown, Mangelsdorf, and Neff 2012). There is evidence to support how a negative father-child attachment affects children negatively in the areas of child development, academic performance, psychological and emotional functioning, and delinquency behaviors.

The purpose of this book is also to investigate the impact on children who do not have a secure father-child attachment. According to Bowlby's attachment theory, if a child does not have a secure father-child attachment or relationship with his or her father, the child could struggle with many negative clinical implications. The focus of this book was primarily on the father-child attachment and the results of not having a secure father-child attachment on children. With the results and information that have been found, clinical providers can use this information in assessing and treating children, adolescents, and adults who have experienced insecure father-child attachment.

It is important to note and consider the differences between correlational relationships and cause-and-effect relationships when looking at the results of data and research that are included in this project. Much of the literature that was reviewed concluded that the data, research, and studies that looked at father-child attachment are mostly correlational in the findings and conclusions. Many studies have found correlations between father-child attachment and child development, academic achievement, emotional and psychological functioning, and legal or delinquency issues with children without a positive father-child attachment. Therefore, future studies and research will be needed to see if any causational data can be found.

This book discusses and identifies various father-child attachment concerns that affect a child's development. For example, when looking at female biological development, it has been found that girls who grow up in homes without their biological fathers tend to go through puberty earlier than their peers. Girls whose early family experiences are characterized by discordant male-female relationships and relatively low paternal investment register that male parental investment is not crucial to reproduction. These girls are hypothesized to develop in a manner that speeds rates of pubertal maturation, accelerates onset of sexual activity, and orients the individual toward relatively unstable pair bonds (James et al. 2012). One can argue that the results in this study can be a result of correlational effect. Fatherless homes can have some correlational effects on biological effects, which can cause girls to experience earlier puberty than girls who have fathers residing in their home.

Also, father involvement and father-child secure attachment has been associated with decreased child's injury risk. Father absence at any point prior to the child's fifteenth birthday was associated with a mortality rate of more than 45 percent, as compared with a mortality rate of 20 percent for children whose father resides with them until their fifteenth birthday (Geary 2000). The presence of a father and the opportunity for a positive father-child attachment can allow for the decrease of child-mortality rates in a society where there are high rates of positive father-child attachment.

Three-year-old children benefit from father involvement with more advanced language development. Poor father-child attachment has been known to establish enduring dysregulations in the child's physiological stress response, promoting pathophysiology in the brain and body and contributing to hypertension, heart disease, infectious disease, and other illnesses (Fabricius and Luecken 2007). Once again the results in these studies can be correlational rather than causational. Child injury risk or mortality may not be caused by fatherless homes, but can result due to more correlational factors or effects. The same argument can be made for the child's physiological stress response that can cause physical illnesses for a child.

Also, I found that a lack of father-child attachment does affect a child's academic achievement in a negative manner. Children with secure father-child attachment were found to have better social performance in school and lower rates of school suspensions or behavioral referrals. When looking at academic performance, positive father-child secure attachment also was found to promote school readiness and school adjustment in children. Therefore, children whose fathers used more positive early parental control had higher Performance IQ scores later in development than other children. Also, father involvement was specifically associated with cognitive gains and higher achievement in math and reading. Finally, the study also highlighted that one of the strongest influences of fathers in their children was their child's overall school success. These include less defiance, greater cooperation with teachers, better cognitive functioning, higher grades in math and reading, and greater overall school readiness (Pougnet et al. 2011). These results can also be due to correlational effects of father-child attachment. Having a positive father-child attachment can correlate to a child performing better academically and having a higher IQ than children without positive father-child attachment.

I also found that a lack of father-child attachment negatively affected emotional and psychological functioning. Research has found that children who experience fathers' absence from the home at various points during childhood are more likely than other children to display internalizing problems, such as sadness, social withdrawal, and anxiety, as well as externalizing problems, such as aggression, impulsivity, and hyperactivity (Pougnet et al. 2011). One of the emotional and psychological effects on children with insecure father-child attachment or no father involvement is that of separation anxiety disorder. Also, high-quality parental bonds and adult attachment security serve to help women resist the negative influence of media portrayals by not internalizing the images presented, thereby experiencing greater satisfaction with their body image. Another key finding was that young adults who recalled poor-quality emotional bonds with their parent had developed a negative self-concept (Cheng and Mallinckrodt 2009).

Another interesting behavioral impact on children who lack positive father-child attachment was substance abuse. Substance abuse was found to be an implication of insecure father-child attachment or lack of father involvement in this study. When children are not raised with a biological father, studies have shown that this is associated with significantly increased odds of alcohol abuse. This finding supports that family composition is strongly related to adolescent alcohol abuse. Adolescents who live in single-parent families, or without any biological parents, drink alcohol more frequently and at more dangerous levels than adolescents who live in two-parent families. Two-parent families provide protection against substance abuse through improved supervision. Supervision of young people reduces the interaction with deviant peers and hence reduces exposure to substance use. It has also been found that girls living in single-mother families were more likely to drink at a high-risk level than boys living in single-mother families (Kenny and Schreiner 2009).

The last question that this book looked at was how the lack of father-child attachment can be a risk factor for legal or delinquency issues. Studies have found that a lack of father-child attachment has a negative impact on children's behavioral concerns, which increases the risk for these children to be more involved with delinquency and illegal activity. Parental bonding was found to be related to several indicators of distress among incarcerated adolescents. Therefore, for both males and females, hopelessness was found to be significantly associated with bonding style with the opposite-sex parent. This study discussed how in early adolescence, excessive emotional separation from parents often led to antisocial conduct, in part because it pushed children into contact with deviant peers (Hodges, Finnegan, and Perry 1999).

An interesting finding was that there was a specific association with children's antisocial propensity and the stressful experiences that were caused by parental incarceration. Social modeling pointed out that children, who grew up seeing their parents respond to stressful life events with antisocial behavior were more likely to also have similar antisocial reactions to their disruptive events and were at higher risk for their own incarceration. Also, children with incarcerated parents were at increased risk for antisocial behavior compared with their peers (Murray, Farrington, and Sekol 2012). A devastating finding from the Bureau of Justice Statistics (2010) was that as of 2009 there were a total of 2,284,900 adult jail and prison inmates in the United States. Men represented 82 percent of those incarcerated. These findings highlight the very high rate of children who are currently not residing or having a positive relationship with their father.

The majority of the results of the studies discussed above can be attributed to correlational versus cause-and-effect phenomena. It is not safe to say that in all instances, lack of positive father-child attachment causes the results found in the majority of these studies. Most of the results can be attributed to more correlational effects and results of not having a positive father-child attachment. These results can still reveal impacts on children who lack this positive father-child attachment. Therefore, these results should be able to inform and support the need of positive father-child attachment, as it can have major impacts on the domains that this project reviewed.

Lastly, in my work with children who have been assessed for mental health evaluations, they have reported in their social and developmental histories how they have been affected by a lack of positive father-child attachment. My findings in the literature used for this book show how lack of attachment between a father and his children affects them in several domains. Many of these children have experienced poor academic progress (lower grades in school), mental health concerns (depression and anxiety diagnosis), delinquency and legal involvement, and some physical health concerns due to not having a positive father-child attachment.

Many of these children and youth have been incarcerated in juvenile detention centers and young adult or adult correctional facilities. A main correlation with these children, youth, and adults is that they have not experienced a positive father-child attachment or reported a healthy relationship with their father. Also, in my work with children who lack positive father-child attachment, I have been able to see that they are at higher risk for mental health concerns and need psychotherapy to address these concerns. The majority of these children have reported at intake and during their counseling process that when they lack a positive father-child attachment or lack of a positive father-child relationship, this has correlated to them experiencing internalizing and externalizing distress in their emotional and behavioral functioning.

On the other side of prevention and fatherhood engagement work, I was able to cochair the Hartford, Connecticut, Fatherhood Engagement Leadership Team (FELT) for several years. I was also a member of the State of Connecticut Fatherhood Engagement Community of Practice. The main goal of both organizations is not only to share the current data and research that was highlighted in this project, but also to provide opportunities for fathers to have a positive father-child attachment or build relationships with their children. Many fathers who have participated in both the Hartford FELT and CT Fatherhood Engagement Community of Practice have been able to understand the importance that positive father-child attachment has for their children. Both organizations have also been able to work with the Connecticut Department of Corrections in order to allow incarcerated fathers to maintain a positive relationship and attachment with their children. This includes providing for flexible visiting arrangements; providing child-friendly visiting rooms with toys, books, and other child-appropriate items; and even allowing fathers to record themselves reading a book so that recorded CD could be provided to their children to listen to their father's voice at home. This would allow the children to maintain a positive attachment with their incarcerated father. This project was called "The Baby Elmo Project."

• • •

Chapter 5

● ● ●

Implications for Practice and Future Research

*"Good fathers do three things: They
provide, they nurture and they guide."*

— ROLAND WARREN

I have found that fathers are unlikely to seek out
treatment because doing so suggests that these
fathers lack appropriate parenting skills. I have also
found that calling an intervention "parent training"
might discourage father participation because the
title implies a skills deficit. Therefore, mental health
providers should consider how they suggest or invite
fathers to attend recommended parental education.

Framing behavior parenting training as a means of enhancing existing skill areas and using a less pejorative label might be better received by fathers. Also, changing the treatment setting from a classroom or didactic setting to one that includes an activity-oriented setting might allow regular attendance for treatment reinforcement and promote the practice of parenting skills. Finally, mental health providers will need to be creative in order to get fathers to participate in treatment for their child and for themselves.

• • •

Direction for Future Research

Future studies and research should include an in-depth look at the differences of academic functioning in boys or girls who do not have a positive father-child attachment. This project has reviewed the effects on academic functioning and even how positive father-child attachment affects the IQ scores of these children. Future research should focus on how father-child attachment affects boys and girls independently. Some research has shown that reading levels are affected differently between girls and boys when they have a negative father-child attachment. Therefore, a more detailed look at these differences in academic functioning is important in order to assist educational professionals in the instruction or support services that may be needed for children who have a negative father-child attachment.

Future research should also look at how medication management and therapeutic intervention can treat individuals with poor father-child attachment. This would include what types of therapeutic modalities are effective in treating individuals with negative father-child attachment. Also, if recommended for medication therapy, future research can provide more clarification on what psychotropic medications are the most effective in working with individuals with a negative father-child attachment. This will allow clinical professionals to create the most appropriate therapeutic interventions for children and adults who have experienced negative father-child attachment.

Future studies should also address if there are any effects on adults' ability to maintain positive relationships such as a couple relationship or marital relationship. I have found that children who have a negative father-child attachment have poorer social skills and peer interactions. Future research can provide more information if this would also affect how children and adults form peer, couple, or even marital relationships. Other areas that can be addressed in future relationship studies include if couple or marital relationships have a better satisfaction rate or lower divorce rate than those with individuals who had a positive father-child attachment experience.

Finally, future research should focus on how fathers who are incarcerated can have a better relationship with their children while incarcerated. There are various programs that incarcerated fathers can participate in. Some of these include educational programs such as GED and community college accredited courses that will allow these men and fathers to achieve a high school diploma or receive further postsecondary educational and vocational services. Some prisons also offer parent education programs of various degrees.

One exciting program that I have been made aware of is a program where fathers who are incarcerated can record audiotapes of themselves reading children's books so that their children can hear their father's voice even if they are incarcerated. Programs such as these and other ways that fathers can maintain some type of relationship with their children may be very beneficial to maintain a father-child relationship.

• • •

Definitions of Terms

Attachment: An enduring affectionate bond that may be signaled by feelings of security, trust, good communication, and acceptance (Arbona and Power 2003, 40).

Accessibility: Potential availability for interaction resulting from the parent's presence whether or not direct interaction is occurring (Willerton et al. 2011, 521).

Avoidance: A desire for emotional separation from parents and lack of security and positive affect in the parent (Arbona and Power 2003, 49).

Engagement: Characterized by undivided attention or direct interaction for an individual (Bouchard 2012, 748).

Family Systems Theory: Families consist of interdependent components or subsystems that exert influence on one another such as mother-father, mother-child, and father-child (Fagan and Cabrera 2012, 1004).

Father Hunger: The emotional and psychological longing that a person has for a father who has been physically, emotionally, or psychologically distant (Perrin et al. 2009, 314).

Insecure Attachment: When infants experience caregivers as inconsistently responsive to or consistently rejecting of the infant's natural proximity-seeking needs (Mattanah, Lopez, and Govern 2011, 566).

Paternal Investment Theory: This integrated model articulates sex-specific pathways linking father presence-absence and stressors in and around the family to pubertal maturation, self-perceived mate value, timing of sexual debut, and sexual risk taking (James et al. 2012, 687).

Pro-social Behaviors: Facilitate smooth interactions or relationships with peers (Attili, Vermigli, and Roazzi 2010, 24).

Responsibility: Overseeing the welfare and care of the child, including organizing and arranging children's lives (Willerton et al. 2011, 521).

Secure Attachment: When infants experience their primary caregivers as consistently warm, accessible, and responsive to their bids for care and support (Mattanah, Lopez, and Govern 2011, 566).

Sensitivity: Refers to parents' ability to recognize and accurately interpret their children's signals, and respond in ways that are affectionate, well timed, and appropriately stimulating (Brown, Mangelsdorf, and Neff 2012, 422).

Social Learning Theory: Emphasizes learning by observation, modeling, and the reinforcement of social interaction patterns in the family context (Bouchard 2012, 748).

References

Arbona, C., and T. Power. 2003. "Parental Attachment, Self-Esteem, and Antisocial Behaviors among African-American, European American, and Mexican American Adolescents." *Journal of Counseling Psychology* 50 (1): 40–51. https://doi.org/10.1037/0022-0167.50.1.40.

Attili, G., P. Vermigli, and A. Roazzi. 2010. "Children's Social Competence, Peer Status, and the Quality of Mother-Child and Father-Child Relationships." *European Psychologist* 15 (1): 23–33. https://doi.org/10.1027/1016-9040/a000002.

Bakermans-Kranenburg, M. J, M. H. Van IJzendoorn, C. L. Bokhorst, and C. Schuegel. 2004. "The Importance of Shared Environment in Infant-Father Attachment: A Behavioral Genetic Study of Attachment Q-Sort." *Journal of Family Psychology* 18 (3): 545–49. https://doi.org/10.1037/0893-3200.18.3.545.

Blazina, C., and C. Watkins Jr. 2000. "Separation/Individuation, Parental Attachment, and Male Gender Role Conflict: Attitudes toward the Feminine and the Fragile Masculine Self." *Psychology of Men & Masculinity* 1 (2): 126–32. https://doi.org/10.1037/1524-9220.1.2.126.

Bouchard, G. 2012. "Intergenerational Transmission and Transition to Fatherhood: A Mediated-Moderation Model of Paternal Engagement." *Journal of Family Psychology* 26 (5): 747–55. https://doi.org/10.1037/a0029391.

Braungart-Rieker, J., S. Courtney, and M. Garwood. 1999. "Mother and Father Infant Attachment: Families in Context." *Journal of Family Psychology* 13 (4): 535–53. https://doi.org/0893-3200/99/.

Braungart-Rieker, J., and J. Karrass. 1999. "Parent Protection in Context." *Journal of Family Psychology* 13 (4): 488–91. https://doi.org/0893-3200/99/.

Brown, G. L., S. C. Mangelsdorf, and C. Neff. 2012. "Father Involvement, Paternal Sensitivity, and Father-Child Attachment Security in the

First 3 Years." *Journal of Family Psychology* 26 (3): 421–30. https://doi.org/10.1037/a0027836.

Byrd-Craven, J., B. J. Auer, D. A. Granger, and A. R. Massey. 2012. "The Father-Daughter Dance: The Relationship between Father-Daughter Relationship Quality and Daughters' Stress Response." *Journal of Family Psychology* 26 (1): 87–94. https://doi.org/10.1037/a0026588.

Cabrera, N. J., R. M. Ryan, S. J. Mitchell, J. D. Shannon, and C. S. Tamis-LeMonda. 2008. "Low-Income, Nonresident Father Involvement with Their Toddlers: Variations by Fathers' Race and Ethnicity." *Journal of Family Psychology* 22 (3): 643–47. https://doi.org/10.1037/0893-3200.22.3.643.

Caldera, Y. M., and E. W. Lindsey. 2006. "Co-parenting, Mother-Infant Interaction, and Infant-Parent Attachment Relationships in Two-Parent Families." *Journal of Family Psychology* 20 (2): 275–83. https://doi.org/10.1037/0893-3200.20.2.275.

Cheng, H-L., and B. Mallinckrodt. 2009. "Parental Bonds, Anxious Attachment, Media Internalization, and

Body Image Dissatisfaction: Exploring a Mediation Model." *Journal of Counseling Psychology* 56 (3): 365–75. https://doi.org/10.1037/a0015067.

Clark, C. D. 2012. "Tough Love: A Brief Cultural History of the Addiction Intervention." *History of Psychology* 15 (3): 233–46. https://doi.org/10.1037/a0025649.

Clarke-Stewart, K. A., D. L. Vandell, K. McCartney, M. T. Owen, and C. Booth. 2000. "Effects of Parental Separation and Divorce on Very Young Children." *Journal of Family Psychology* 14 (2): 304–26. https://doi.org/10.1037//0893-3200.14.2.304.

Connell, A. M., T. J. Dishion, M. Yasui, and K. Kavanagh. 2007. "An Adaptive Approach to Family Intervention: Linking Engagement in Family-Centered Intervention to Reductions in Adolescent Problem Behavior." *Journal of Consulting and Clinical Psychology* 75 (4): 568–79. https://doi.org/10.1037/0022-006X.75.4.568.

Cronk, N. J., W. S. Slutske, P. A. F. Madden, K. K. Bucholz, and A. C. Heath. 2004. "Risk for Separation Anxiety Disorder among Girls:

Paternal Absence, Socioeconomic Disadvantages, and Genetic Vulnerability." *Journal of Abnormal Psychology* 113 (2): 237–47. https://doi.org/10.1037/0021-843X.113.2.237.

Cruz, R. A., K. M. King, K. F. Widaman, J. Leu, A. M. Cauce, and R. D. Conger. 2011. "Cultural Influences on Positive Father Involvement in Two-Parent Mexican-Origin Families." *Journal of Family Psychology* 25 (5): 731–40. https://doi.org/10.1037/a0025128.

Day, R. D., and L. M. Padilla-Walker. 2009. "Mother and Father Connectedness and Involvement during Early Adolescence." *Journal of Family Psychology* 23 (6): 900–4. https://doi.org/10.1037/a0016438.

DeFranc, W., and J. R. Mahalik. 2002. "Masculine Gender Role Conflict and Stress in Relation to Parental Attachment and Separation." *Psychology of Men & Masculinity* 3 (1): 51–60. https://doi.org/10.1037//1524-9220.3.1.51.

Dykas, M. J., and J. Cassidy. 2011. "Attachment and the Processing of Social Information across the Life

Span: Theory and Evidence." *Psychology Bulletin* 137 (1): 19–46. https://doi.org/10.1037/a0021367.

Ellis, B. J. 2004. "Timing of Pubertal Maturation in Girls: An Integrated Life History Approach." *Psychological Bulletin* 130 (6): 920–58. https://doi.org/10.1037/0033-2909.130.6.920.

Fabiano, G. A. 2007. "Father Participation in Behavioral Parent Training for ADHD: Review and Recommendations for Increasing Inclusion and Engagement." *Journal of Family Psychology* 21 (4): 683–93. https://doi.org/10.1037/0893-3200.21.4.683.

Fabricius, W. V., and L. J. Luecken. 2007. "Postdivorce Living Arrangements, Parent Conflict, and Long-Term Physical Health Correlates for Children of Divorce." *Journal of Family Psychology* 21 (2): 195–205. https://doi.org/10.1037/0893-3200.21.2.195.

Fagan, J., and N. Cabrera. 2012. "Longitudinal and Reciprocal Associations between Co-parenting Conflict and Father Engagement." *Journal of Family Psychology* 26 (6): 1004–11. https://doi.org/10.1037/a0029998.

References

Fagan, J., and R. Palkovitz. 2007. "Unmarried, Nonresident Fathers' Involvement with Their Infants: A Risk and Resilience Perspective." *Journal of Family Psychology* 21 (3): 479–89. https://doi.org/10.1037/0893-3200.21.3.479.

Fagan, J., R. Palkovitz, K. Roy, and D. Farrie. 2009. "Pathways to Paternal Engagement: Longitudinal Effects of Risk and Resilience on Nonresident Fathers." *Developmental Psychology* 45 (5): 1389–405. https://doi.org/10.1037/a0015210.

Feldman, R., and S. Masalha. 2010. "Parent-Child and Antecedents of Children's Social Competence: Cultural Specificity, Shared Process." *Developmental Psychology* 46 (2): 455–67. https://doi.org/10.1037/a0017415.

Fleming, L. M., and D. J. Tobin. 2005. "Popular Child-Rearing Books: Where Is Daddy?" *Psychology of Men & Masculinity* 6 (1): 18–24. https://doi.org/10.1037/1524-9220.6.1.18.

Furman, W., and V. A. Simon. 2004. "Concordance in Attachment States of Mind and Styles with

Respect to Fathers and Mothers." *Developmental Psychology* 40 (6): 1239–47. https://doi.org/10.1037/0012-1649.40.6.1239.

Ganiban, J. M., J. Ulbricht, K. J. Saudino, D. Reiss, and J. M. Neiderhiser. 2011. "Understanding Child-Based Effects on Parenting: Temperament as a Moderator of Genetics and Environmental Contributions to Parenting." *Developmental Psychology* 47 (3): 676–92. https://doi.org/10.1037/a0021812.

Garfield, C. F., and A. J. Isacco III. 2012. "Urban Fathers' Involvement in Their Child's Health and Healthcare." *Psychology of Men & Masculinity* 13 (1): 32–48. https://doi.org/10.1037/a0025696.

Geary, D. C. 2000. "Evolution and Proximate Expression of Human Paternal Investment." *Psychological Bulletin* 126 (1): 55–77. https://doi.org/10.1037/0033-2909.126.1.55.

Gee, C. B., and J. E. Rhodes. 2003. "Adolescent Mothers' Relationship with Their Children's Biological Fathers: Social Support, Social Strain, and Relationship Continuity." *Journal of*

Family Psychology 17 (3): 370–83. https://doi.org/10.1037/0893-3200.17.3.370.

Goodyear, R. K., M. D. Newcomb, and T. F. Locke. 2002. "Pregnant Latina Teenagers: Psychosocial and Developmental Determinants of How They Select and Perceive the Men Who Father Their Children." *Journal of Counseling Psychology* 49 (2): 187–201. https://doi.org/10.1037//0022-0167.49.2.187.

Gordon, D. M., S. W. Hawes, M. A. Perez-Cabello, Brabham-Hollis, A. S. Lanza, and W. J. Dyson. 2013. "Examining Masculine Norms and Peer Support within a Sample of Incarcerated African-American Males." *Psychology of Men & Masculinity* 14 (1): 59–64. https://doi.org/10.1037/a0028780.

Haavind, H. 2011. "Loving and Caring for Small Children: Contested Issues for Everyday Practices." *Nordic Psychology* 63 (2): 24–48. https://doi.org/10.1027/1901-2276/a000031.

Henry, K. L. 2008. "Low Pro-social Attachment, Involvement with Drug Using Peers, and Adolescent Drug Use: A Longitudinal Examination of

Meditational Mechanisms." *Psychology of Addictive Behaviors* 22 (2): 302–8. https://doi.org/10.1037/0893-164X.22.2.302.

Hodges, E. V. E., R. A. Finnegan, and D. G. Perry. 1999. "Skewed Autonomy-Relatedness in Preadolescents' Conceptions of Their Relationships with Mother, Father, and Best Friend." *Developmental Psychology* 35 (3): 737–48. https://doi.org/0012-1649/99/.

Howard, K. S., J. E. Burke Lefever, J. G. Borkowski, and T. L. Whitman. 2006. "Fathers' Influence in the Lives of Children with Adolescent Mothers." *Journal of Family Psychology* 20 (3): 468–76. https://doi.org/10.1037/ 0893-3200.20.3.468.

Iwamoto, D. K, D. M. Gordon, A. Oliveros, M. A. Perez-Cabello, T. Brabham, A. S. Lanza, and W. Dyson. 2012. "The Role of Masculine Norms and Informal Support on Mental Health in Incarcerated Men." *Psychology of Men & Masculinity* 13 (3): 283–93. https://doi.org/10.1037/a0025522.

James, J., B. J. Ellis, G. L. Schlomer, and J. Garber. 2012. "Sex-Specific Pathways to Early Puberty, Sexual Debut, and Sexual Risk Taking: Tests of an Integrated Evolutionary-Developmental Model." *Developmental Psychology* 48 (3): 687–702. https://doi.org/10.1037/a0026427.

Jia, R., L. E. Kotila, and S. J. Schoppe-Sullivan. 2012. "Transactional Relations between Father Involvement and Preschoolers' Socioemotional Adjustment." *Journal of Family Psychology* 26 (6): 848–57. https://doi.org/10.1037/a0030245.

Kelly, J. B., and M. E. Lamb. 2003. "Developmental Issues in Relocation Cases Involving Young Children: When, Whether, and How?" *Journal of Family Psychology* 17 (2): 193–205. https://doi.org/10.1037/0893-3200.17.2.193.

Kenny, D. T., and I. Schreiner. 2009. "Predictors of High-Risk Alcohol Consumption in Young Offenders on Community Orders: Policy and Treatment Implications." *Psychology, Public Policy, and Law* 15 (1): 54–79. https://doi.org/10.1037/a0015079.

Kenny, M. C. 2000. "Working with Children of Divorce and Their Family." *Psychotherapy* 37 (3): 228–39.

Kerns, K. A., P. L. Tomich, J. E. Aspelmeier, and J. M. Contreras. 2000. "Attachment-Based Assessments of Parent-Child Relationships in Middle Childhood." *Developmental Psychology* 36 (5): 614–26. https://doi.org/10.1037//0012-1649.36.5.614.

Kochanska, G., N. Aksan, and J. J. Carlson. 2005. "Temperament, Relationships, and Young Children's Receptive Cooperation with Their Parents." *Developmental Psychology* 41 (4): 648–60. https://doi.org/10.1037/0012-1649.41.4.648.

Kotila, L. E., and C. M. Kamp Dush. 2012. "Another Baby? Father Involvement and Childbearing in Fragile Families." *Journal of Family Psychology* 26 (6): 976–86. https://doi.org/10.1037/a0030715.

Krishnakumar, A., and M. M. Black. 2003. "Family Processes within Three-Generation Households and Adolescent Mothers' Satisfaction with Father Involvement." *Journal of Family Psychology* 17 (4): 488–98. https://doi.org/10.1037/0893-3200.17.4.488.

Laurent, H. K., H. K. Kim, and D. M. Capaldi. 2008. "Prospective Effects of Interparental Conflict on Child Attachment Security and the Moderating

Role of Parents' Romantic Attachment." *Journal of Family Psychology* 22 (3): 377–88. https://doi.org/10.1037/0893-3200.22.3.377.

Lindsey, E. W., Y. M. Caldera, and L. Tankersley. 2009. "Marital Conflict and the Quality of Young Children's Peer Play Behavior: The Mediating and Moderating Role of Parent-Child Emotional Reciprocity and Attachment Security." *Journal of Family Psychology* 23 (2): 130–45. https://doi.org/10.1037/a0014972.

Lucassen, N., A. Tharner, M. H. Van IJzendoorn, M. J. Bakermans-Kranenburg, B. L. Volling, F. C. Verhulst, M. P. Lambregtse-Van den Berg, and H. Tiemeier. 2011. "The Association between Paternal Sensitivity and Infant-Father Attachment Security: A Meta-analysis of Three Decades of Research." *Journal of Family Psychology* 25 (6): 986–92. https://doi.org/10.1037/a0025855.

Mackey, W. C. 2001. "Support for the Existence of an Independent Man-to-Child Affiliative Bond: Fatherhood as a Biocultural Invention." *Psychology of Men & Masculinity* 2 (1): 51–66. https://doi.org/10.1037//1524-9220.2.1.51.

Madsen, S. A., D. Lind, and H. Munck. 2007. "Men's Abilities to Reflect Their Infants' States of Mind." *Nordic Psychology* 59 (2): 149–63.

Magaletta, P. R., and D. P. Herbst. 2001. "Fathering from Prison: Common Struggles and Successful Solutions." *Psychotherapy* 38 (1): 88–96.

Martin, A., R. M. Ryan, and J. Brooks-Gunn. 2010. "When Fathers' Supportiveness Matters Most: Maternal and Paternal Parenting and Children's School Readiness." *Journal of Family Psychology* 24 (2): 145–55. https://doi.org/10.1037/a0018073.

Mattanah, J. F., F. G. Lopez, and J. M. Govern. 2012. "The Contributions of Parental Attachment Bonds to College Student Development and Adjustment: A Meta-analytic Review." *Journal of Counseling Psychology* 58 (4): 565–96. https://doi.org/ 10.1037/a0024635.

McGarvey, E. L., L. A. Kryzhanovskaya, C. Koopman, D. Waite, and R. J. Canterbury. 1999. "Incarcerated Adolescents' Distress and Suicidality in Relation to Parental Bonding Styles." *The Journal of Crisis Intervention and Suicide Prevention* 20 (4): 164–70.

Mills-Koonce, W. R., P. Garrett-Peters, M. Barnett, D. A. Granger, C. Blair, M. J. Cox, and Family Life Project Key Investigators. 2011. "Father Contributions to Cortisol Responses in Infancy and Toddlerhood." *Developmental Psychology* 47 (2): 388–95. https://doi.org/10.1037/a0021066.

Murray, J., D. P. Farrington, and I. Sekol. 2012. "Children's Antisocial Behavior, Mental Health, Drug Use, and Educational Performance after Parental Incarceration: A Systematic Review and Meta-analysis." *Psychological Bulletin* 138 (2): 175–210. https://doi.org/10.1037/a0026407.

Nettle, D., W. E. Frankenhuis, and I. J. Rickard. 2012. "The Adaptive Basis of Psychosocial Acceleration: Comment on Beyond Mental Health, Life History Strategies Articles." *Developmental Psychology* 48 (3): 718–21. https://doi.org/10.1037/a0027507.

Nixon, E., S. Greene, and D. Hogan. 2012. "Like an Uncle but More, but Less Than a Father—Irish Children's Relationships with Nonresident Fathers." *Journal of Family Psychology* 26 (3): 381–90. https://doi.org/10.1037/a0028336.

Papp, L. M., E. M. Cummings, and M. C. Goeke-Morey. 2002. "Marital Conflicts in the Home When Children Are Present versus Absent." *Developmental Psychology* 38 (5): 774–83. https://doi.org/10.1037//0012-1649.38.5.774.

Pears, K. C., H. K. Kim, D. Capaldi, D. C. Kerr, and P. A. Fisher. 2012. "Father-Child Transmission of School Adjustment: A Prospective Inter-generational Study." *Developmental Psychology* 21 (1): 1–12. https://doi.org/10.1037/a0028543.

Perrin, P. B., J. O. Baker, A. M. Romelus, K. D. Jones, and M. Heesacker. 2009. "Development, Validation, and Confirmatory Factor Analysis of the Father Hunger Scale." *Psychology of Men & Masculinity* 10 (4): 314–27. https://doi.org/10.1037/a0017277.

Pougnet, E., L. A. Serbin, D. M. Stack, and A. E. Schwartzman. 2011. "Fathers' Influence on Children's Cognitive and Behavioral Functioning: A Longitudinal Study of Canadian Families." *Canadian Journal of Behavioural Science* 43 (3): 173–82. https://doi.org/10.1037/a0023948.

Rosenberg, T., and C. G. Shields. 2009. "The Role of Parent-Adolescent Attachment in the Glycemic Control of Adolescents with Type 1 Diabetes: A Pilot Study." *Families, Systems, & Health* 27 (3): 237–48. https://doi.org/10.1037/a0017117.

Rouyer, V., F. Franscarolo, C. Zaouche-Gaudron, and C. Lavanchy. 2007. "Fathers of Girls, Fathers of Boys: Influence of Child's Gender on Fathers' Experience of, Engagement in, and Representations of Paternity." *Swiss Journal of Psychology* 66 (4): 225–33. https://doi.org/10.1024/1421-0185.66.4.225.

Schacht, P. M., E. M. Cummings, and P. T. Davies. 2009. "Fathering in Family Context and Child Adjustment: A Longitudinal Analysis." *Journal of Family Psychology* 23 (6): 790–97. https://doi.org/10.1037/a0016741.

Schindler, H. S., and R. Levine Coley. 2012. "Predicting Marital Separation: Do Parent-Child Relationships Matter?" *Journal of Family Psychology* 26 (4): 499–508. https://doi.org/10.1037/a0028863.

Schneider-Rosen, K., and P. B. Burke. 1999. "Multiple Attachment Relationships within Families: Mother and Fathers with Two Young Children." *Developmental Psychology* 35 (2): 436–44. https://doi.org/0012-1649/99/.

Schwebel, D. C., and C. M. Brezausek. 2007. "Father Transitions in the Household and Young Children's Injury Risk." *Psychology of Men & Masculinity* 8 (3): 173–84. https://doi.org/10.1037/1524-9220.8.3.173.

Sheeber, L. B., B. Davis, C. Leve, H. Hops, and E. Tildesley. 2007. "Adolescents' Relationships with Their Mothers and Fathers: Associations with Depressive Disorder and Subdiagnostic Symptomology." *Journal of Abnormal Psychology* 116 (1): 144–54. https://doi.org/10.1037/0021-843X.116.1.144.

Silverstein, L. B., and C. F. Auerbach. 1999. "Deconstructing the Essential Father." *American Psychologist* 54 (6): 397–407. https://doi.org/0003-066X/99/.

Strenger, C. 2004. "Identity Formation in a Fatherless Generation." *Psychoanalytic Psychology* 21 (4): 499–515. https://doi.org/10.1037/0736-9735.21.4.499.

Taylor, E. 2000. "Psychotherapeutics and the Problematic Origins of Clinical Psychology in America." *American Psychologist* 55 (9): 1029–33. https://doi.org/10.1037//0003-066X.55.9.1029.

Timmons-Fritz, P. A., A. M. Smith-Slep, and K. D. O'Leary. 2012. "Couple-Level Analysis of the Relation between Family-of-Origin Aggression and Intimate Partner Violence." *Psychology of Violence* 2 (2): 139–53. https://doi.org/10.1037/a0027370.

Tither, J. M., and B. J. Ellis. 2008. "Impact of Fathers on Daughters' Age at Menarche: A Genetically and Environmentally Controlled Sibling Study." *Developmental Psychology* 44 (5): 1409–20. https://doi.org/10.1037/a0013065.

US Department of Justice. 2011. "Prison Statistics." http://bjs.ojp.usdoj.gov/content/pub/pdf/mhp-pji.pdf.

Vigil, J. M., and D. C. Geary. 2006. "Parenting and Community Background and Variation in Women's Life-History Development." *Journal of*

Family Psychology 20 (4): 597–604. https://doi.org/10.1037/0893-3200.20.4.597.

Willerton, E., R. L. Schwartz, S. M. MacDermid Wadsworth, and M. Schultheis Oglesby. 2011. "Military Fathers' Perspectives on Involvement." *Journal of Family Psychology* 25 (4): 521–30. https://doi.org/10.1037/a0024511.

Wong, M. S., S. C. Mangelsdorf, G. L. Brown, C. Neff, and S. J. Schoppe-Sullivan. 2009. "Parental Beliefs, Infant Temperament, and Marital Quality: Associations with Infant-Mother and Infant-Father Attachment." *Journal of Family Psychology* 23 (6): 828–38. https://doi.org/10.1037/a0016491.

Zvizdic, S., and W. Butollo. 2000. "War-Related Loss of One's Father and Persistent Depressive Reactions in Early Adolescents." *European Psychologist* 5 (3): 204–14.

• • •

For more information about Dr. Noel Casiano or for invitations for keynote speaking events, conferences, workshops and other events, please contact us at:
www.drnoelcasiano.com
email: casianoclinicalservices@gmail.com

• • •

Follow Dr. Noel Casiano on social media:
Facebook: Casiano Clinical Services, LLC
Twitter: @noelcasiano
Instagram: @dr.noel.casiano

51697739R00074

Made in the USA
Columbia, SC
20 February 2019